Zeal

A Bible Study on Titus for Women

Keri Folmar

To my son, Andrew:
May you hold firm to the trustworthy word as taught.

– Keri Folmar

CruciformPress

Praise for Keri Folmar's Inductive Bible Studies for Women

"With simple clarity, Keri Folmar guides us in learning to study the Bible…Keri encourages us to read God's Word carefully, to understand clearly, and to apply prayerfully…she encourages her readers first and foremost to listen well to God's inspired Word."

Kathleen Nielson is author of the *Living Word Bible Studies*; Director of Women's Initiatives, The Gospel Coalition; and wife of Niel, who served as President of Covenant College, 2002 to 2012.

"Keri's Bible study will not only bring the truths of [Scripture] to bear upon your life, but will also train you up for better, more effective study of any book of the Bible with her consistent use of the three questions needed in all good Bible study: Observation, Interpretation, and Application."

Connie Dever is author of *The Praise Factory* children's ministry curriculum and wife of Mark, senior pastor of Capitol Hill Baptist Church and President of 9Marks.

"It is hard to imagine a better inductive Bible study tool than this one. So many study tools wander from the biblical text, but Keri Folmar's study concentrates on what [the biblical author] says… unfolding its message with accuracy and clarity."

Diane Schreiner, the wife of SBTS professor, author, and pastor Tom Schreiner and mother of four grown children, has led women's Bible studies for more than 20 years.

"No clever stories, ancillary anecdotes, or emotional manipulation here. Keri takes us deeper into the text, deeper into the heart of [the biblical author], deeper into the mind of Christ, and deeper into our own hearts… a great study to do on your own or with others."

Kristie Anyabwile is a North Carolina native and graduate of NC State University with a degree in history. Her husband, Thabiti, serves as a pastor in Washington, DC, and as a Council Member for The Gospel Coalition.

"Keri is convinced that God is God-centered and that for the sake of our joy, we should be, too…She skillfully created these rich resources—and not only that, she has put the tools in your hands so you can study God's word for yourself…I highly recommend that you embark on these studies with some other ladies. Then you can all watch in amazement at how God gives you contentment in him."

Gloria Furman is a pastor's wife in the Middle East, and author of *Glimpses of Grace, Treasuring Christ When Your Hands Are Full,* and *The Pastor's Wife.*

Table of Contents

We offer five more Bible studies for women from Keri Folmar, including these…

JOY!
A Bible Study on Philippians
for Women

bit.ly/JoyStudy

FAITH:
A Bible Study on James
for Women

bit.ly/FaithStudy

CruciformPress.com

Zeal - A Bible Study on Titus for Women

Print / PDF ISBN: 978-1-941114-80-3

As we begin this study of Paul's letter to Titus, we should think through why we are studying the Bible. Why not read some other book? Or why not just get together with some other women and chat?

Well, have you heard the story about the kindergarten teacher who had her class paint pictures of anything they chose? After observing a little girl who was working very intently on her painting, the teacher asked, "What are you painting?" The girl answered, "It's a picture of God." Amused, the teacher informed her, "No one knows what God looks like." Without looking up from her painting, the little girl responded, "They will in a minute!"

This might be a cute example of a precocious child, but many people paint pictures of God in their own minds. They "know" that God is a certain way, because they want him to be that way.

However, the one true God is transcendent. He is beyond our capacity to know. First Timothy 6:16 describes God, "[W]ho alone has immortality, who dwells in unapproachable light, whom no one has ever seen or can see." God existed before time. He is the Creator, and we are his creatures. Sinful man cannot approach the holy God.

How can we know this God if we cannot approach him? He has to approach us. The only way to truly know God is for him to reveal himself to us. He reveals his existence and power in creation. (See Psalm 19 and Romans 1:18–21.) However, if we want to truly know God in a personal way, it must be through his Word.

And God *wants* us, his creatures, to know him. Jeremiah 10:23–24 says:

> Thus says the Lord: "Let not the wise man boast in his wisdom, let not the mighty man boast in his might, let not the rich man boast in his riches, but let him who boasts boast in this, that he understands and knows me, that I am the Lord who practices steadfast love, justice, and righteousness in the earth."

Do you boast in understanding and knowing the Lord? Do you want to know this God who practices love, justice, and righteousness in the earth? He wants you to understand and know him. He is ready to speak to you every morning when you wake up… throughout the day… and before you go to bed. You have only to open his Word.

A well-known catechism says, "The chief end of man is to glorify God and enjoy him forever." That is what we were created for—to truly know and enjoy the God of the universe. Jeremiah the prophet cried out: "Your words were found, and I ate them, and your words became to me a joy and the delight of my heart."

The great preacher, CH Spurgeon, said:

> Believer! There is enough in the Bible for you to live upon forever. If you should outnumber the years of Methuselah, there would be no need for a fresh revelation; if you should live until Christ should return to the earth, there would be no necessity for the addition of a single word; if you should go down as deep as Jonah, or even descend as David said he did, into the depths of hell, still there would be enough in the Bible to comfort you without a supplementary sentence. (http://spurgeon.org/sermons/0005.htm)

This is why we study the Bible: it is God's revelation of himself to us. We need to know who God truly is and guard against painting our own picture of him. God has revealed himself to us not in paintings but through his Son by the words of the Scripture. God, the Creator, has spoken, and we, his creation, should listen to his words as life-sustaining truth and joyfully obey them.

This Bible study workbook is to assist you in studying Titus in an inductive way. Inductive study is **reading the passage in context and asking questions of the text with the purpose of deriving the meaning and significance from the text itself.** We do this automatically every day when we read the newspaper, blogs, or even recipes. When we study the Bible inductively we are after the author's original intent; i.e., what the author meant when he wrote the passage to his original audience. In this workbook, you will figure out the meaning by answering a series of questions about the text, paying close attention to the words and context of the passage. After figuring out the meaning of the text, there will be questions to help you apply it to your life.

As you read through Titus, may the Holy Spirit open your eyes to more deeply understand and rejoice in the gospel of Jesus Christ and the church.

How to Do Inductive Bible Study

Step 1 – **Begin with prayer.** "Open my eyes, that I may behold wondrous things out of your law" (Psalm 119:18).

Step 2 – **Read the text.**

Step 3 – **Observation.** *The goal of this step is to figure out what the text is saying.* These questions should be answered from the very words of the text.

Step 4 – **Interpretation.** *The goal of this step is to figure out what the text meant to the original hearers.* This most important step is often skipped, but a lack of correct interpretation leads to incorrect application. We cannot understand what God is saying to us if we don't first understand what he was saying to his original audience, and why he was saying it.

Your job in interpretation is to figure out the main point of the passage and understand the arguments that support the main point. Your interpretation should flow out of your observations, so keep asking yourself, *Can I support this interpretation based on my observations?*

Step 5 – **Application. Prayerfully apply the passage to your own life.** The application should flow from the main point of the text.

Keep God's Redemptive Plan in Mind

Luke 24:44–47 says,

Then [Jesus] said to them, "These are my words that I spoke to you while I was still with you, that everything written about me in the Law of Moses and the Prophets and the Psalms must be fulfilled." Then he opened their minds to understand the Scriptures, and said to them, "Thus it is written, that the Christ should suffer and on the third day rise from the dead, and that repentance and forgiveness of sins should be proclaimed in his name to all nations, beginning from Jerusalem."

We study the Bible so that we can know Christ, repent, be forgiven, and proclaim him to the nations. We must keep Jesus in mind when we study Scripture. Adrienne Lawrence writes, "God has one overarching redemptive plan—to glorify himself by creating and redeeming a people for himself through Christ. Christ is at the center of God's plan. All of Scripture in some way speaks to that plan. Keep this in mind as you are doing your study of Scripture."

[Note: this "How to" has been adapted from Adrienne Lawrence's pamphlet on Inductive Bible Study.]

Notes on This Study Guide

The first week of this inductive study will be an overview of Titus. On the following days you will study smaller segments of the letter and answer observation, interpretation, and application questions. The questions were written based on language from the English Standard Version of the Bible. However, you are welcome to use any reliable translation to do the study.

To assist you in recognizing the different types of questions asked, the questions are set out in three different fonts.

👁 **Observation:**   Look closely at the text to figure out what it is saying. Get answers directly from the text, using the words of Scripture to answer the observation questions.

✦ **Interpretation:**   Determine the author's intended meaning by figuring out what the text meant to its original hearers.

❤ **Application:**   Based on the author's meaning of the text, apply the passage to your own heart and life today.

Because Scripture interprets Scripture, many of the questions cite passages in addition to the one you are studying in Titus. If the question says, "Read…" you will need to read the additional verses cited to answer the question. If the question says, "See…" the verses help you answer the question but are not necessary. "See also…" signals you to read the verses if you would like to study the answer to the question further.

You only need your Bible to do this study of Titus, and, in fact, I highly recommend first answering the questions directly from your Bible before looking at any other materials. That said, it might be helpful for you to confirm your answers, especially if you are leading others in a group study. To check your answers or for further study, *The Message of 1 Timothy & Titus* by John Stott is a good commentary to use. For more detail, use *The Pastoral Epistles* by George W. Knight III.

For more general help in knowing how to study the Bible, I highly recommend *Bible Study: Following the Ways of the Word*, by Kathleen Buswell Nielson and *Dig Deeper! Tools to Unearth the Bible's Treasure*, by Nigel Beynon and Andrew Sach. Bible study teachers and students who want a closer look at New Testament theology that will also encourage your heart can read Thomas Schreiner's, *Magnifying God in Christ: A Summary of New Testament Theology*. For information that explains why Christians base their life and doctrine on the Bible, see my book, *The Good Portion: The Doctrine of Scripture for Every Woman*.

Notes for Leaders

This Bible study can be done by individuals alone, but the best context for Bible study is in the local church. Studying the Bible together promotes unity and ignites spiritual growth within the church.

The study was designed for participants to complete five days of "homework," and then come together to discuss their answers in a small group. The goal of gathering in small groups is to promote discussion among women to sharpen one another by making sure all understand the meaning of the text and can apply it to their lives. As women discuss, their eyes may be opened to applications of the text they didn't see while doing the study on their own. Believers will encourage one another in their knowledge of the gospel, and unbelievers will hear the gospel clearly explained. As a result, women will learn from one another and come away from group Bible study with a deeper understanding of the text and a better knowledge of how to read the Bible on their own in their private times of study and prayer.

If you are leading a small group, you will have some extra homework to do. **First, know what Bible study is and is not.** Bible study is not primarily a place to meet felt needs, eat good food and chat, receive counseling, or have a free-for-all discussion. Some of these things do happen in a women's Bible study, but they should not take over the focus. Bible study is digging into the Scriptures to get the true meaning of the text and applying it to lives that change as a result.

Second, make sure you know the main points of the text before leading discussion by carefully studying the passage and checking yourself using a good commentary, like one of those listed above. You may also find a Bible dictionary and concordance helpful. Second Timothy 3:16–17 says, "All Scripture is breathed out by God and profitable for teaching, for reproof, for correction, and for training in righteousness, that the man [or woman] of God may be competent, equipped for every good work." Scripture is powerful. That power comes through truth. Scripture is not like a magical incantation: We say the words and see the effect. We must know what the text of Scripture means before we apply it and see its work of transformation in our lives. Your job as a discussion leader is not to directly teach, nor to simply facilitate discussion, but rather to lead women in finding the meaning of the text and help them see how it is "profitable" and can make them "competent, equipped for every good work" (2 Timothy 3:16–17).

Third, pray. Pray for the women in your group during the week while you prepare. Pray as you start your small group study, asking the Holy Spirit to illuminate the Scripture to your minds and apply it to your hearts. And encourage women to pray at the end of your small group based on what they studied. Ask the Holy Sprit to use his sword, the word of God, in the lives of the women you are leading.

Fourth, draw women into discussion and keep your discussion organized. Choose what you determine are the most important questions from the study guide, focusing the bulk of your discussion on the interpretation and application questions. Ask a question, but don't answer it! Be comfortable with long pauses or rephrase questions you think the group didn't understand. Not answering the questions yourself may be a bit awkward at first, but it will promote discussion in the end because the women will know they have to do the answering. Feel free to affirm good answers or sum up after women have had time to discuss particular questions. This gives clarity to the discussion. However, don't feel the need to fill in every detail and nuance you gleaned from your personal study. Your goal is to get your group talking.

Fifth, keep your focus on the Bible. The Holy Spirit uses the Scriptures to change women's hearts. Don't be afraid of wrong answers. Gently use them to clarify and teach by directing attention back to the text of Scripture for the right answer. If someone in your group goes off on unhelpful tangents, direct her back to the question and address the tangent later, one on one, or with reading material. However, if the tangent is on a vital question that goes to the gospel, take time to talk about it. These are God-given opportunities.

Sixth, be sure to discuss the gospel. In your prep time, ask yourself what the text has to do with the gospel and look for opportunities to ask questions to bring out the gospel. Hopefully, your church members will invite unbelievers to your study who will hear the glorious good news. But, even if your group is made up of all believers, we never get beyond our need to be reminded of Christ crucified and what that means for our lives.

Lastly, enjoy studying the Scriptures with your group. Your love and passion for the word of God will be contagious, and you will have the great joy of watching your women catch it and rejoice in God's word with you.

Paul's Letter to Titus

The apostle Paul was personally commissioned by Jesus Christ to be an ambassador of the gospel. He traveled with companions all over the Greco-Roman world, planting churches in Asia Minor and along the Mediterranean Sea. Titus was one of Paul's emissaries, his "partner and fellow worker" (2 Corinthians 8:23).

The people of the Mediterranean island of Crete were known for immorality and deceitfulness, but the gospel had taken root there. Paul planted churches in towns on the island and left Titus to oversee the organization of these fledgling gatherings. Paul's letter to Titus is not only a prescription for church governance, but is also a manifesto for the Christian life. It instructs Titus to appoint elders, rebuke false teachers and teach godliness that "accords with sound doctrine" (Tit. 2:1). Along the way, Paul unfolds the good news of Jesus Christ and its implications for the believer.

Titus is a vital book for us today. The church is "a pillar and buttress of the truth" (1 Timothy 3:15). Biblical church governance guards sound doctrine and godly living, protecting and advancing the precious gospel of our Lord and Savior Jesus Christ.

Week 1

Pray this week for the Lord to make you fit for every good work through the study of his word.

Pray, then read through Titus and answer the following questions.

✦ 1. How would you describe the tone of the letter?

👁 2. What words, phrases, or ideas are repeated throughout the letter?

✦ 3. What is the purpose of this letter, and how do you know it is the purpose?

❤ 4. What questions arose in your mind as you read through Titus?

Day 2

Pray, then read Titus 1.

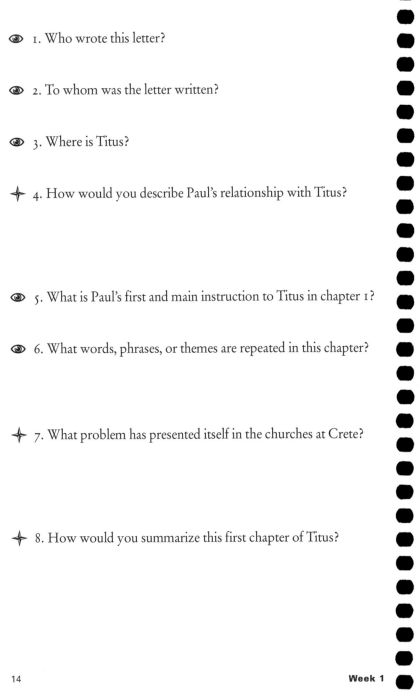

👁 1. Who wrote this letter?

👁 2. To whom was the letter written?

👁 3. Where is Titus?

✦ 4. How would you describe Paul's relationship with Titus?

👁 5. What is Paul's first and main instruction to Titus in chapter 1?

👁 6. What words, phrases, or themes are repeated in this chapter?

✦ 7. What problem has presented itself in the churches at Crete?

✦ 8. How would you summarize this first chapter of Titus?

♥ 9. What questions arose in your mind as you read through Titus 1?

Day 3

Pray, then read Titus 2.

👁 1. What is Paul's first and main instruction to Titus in this chapter?

✦ 2. How does this chapter relate to chapter 1?

👁 3. What words, phrases, or themes are repeated in this chapter?

✦ 4. What stands out to you the most in this chapter?

✦ 5. How would you summarize the theme of this chapter?

♥ 6. What questions arose in your mind as you read through Titus 2?

Day 4

Pray, then read Titus 3.

👁 1. What are Paul's main instructions to Titus in this chapter?

✦ 2. How would you summarize them?

✦ 3. How does this chapter relate to the previous chapters?

👁 4. What words, phrases, or themes are repeated in this chapter?

👁 5. What contrasts do you see?

✦ 6. What stands out to you the most in this chapter?

✦ 7. How would you summarize the theme of this chapter?

♥ 8. What questions arose in your mind as you read through Titus 3?

Day 5

Pray, then read Titus.

✦ 1. Why did Paul write this letter? How do you know his purpose?

✦ 2. How would you sum up the letter in one sentence?

✦ 3. Paul wrote this letter to Titus, a pastor. How can you learn from the letter even though you aren't a pastor?

♥ 4. How do you hope to grow spiritually through studying this letter?

Notes

Week 2

Pray this week for deeper knowledge of the truth, which accords with godliness.

Pray, then read Titus 1:1–5.

Titus 1:1a

👁 1. Who wrote this letter, and how does he describe himself?

✦ 2. What does Paul mean when he calls himself a "servant of God"? See 2 Samuel 7:4; Psalm 105:26; and Jeremiah 7:25. Is it a humble title, an exalted title, or both?

✦ 3. Who was Paul, and what does it mean that he is an "apostle of Jesus Christ"? See Acts 9:1–22; Galatians 1:1 and 15–16; and Ephesians 3:7–9.

✦ 4. What is Paul conveying about himself with these titles?

♥ 5. How should this affect the way we read this letter?

♥ 6. Paul was specially called by God as his servant to take the message of the gospel to the Gentiles. Even though you're not an apostle, do you consider yourself a servant of God? In what ways do you use your time, resources, and talents to serve God?

♥ 7. Would someone observing your life notice that you are a servant of God? What would he or she see?

Day 2

Pray, then read Titus 1:1–5.

Titus 1:1b

👁 1. For what purpose is Paul "a servant of God and an apostle of Jesus Christ"?

✦ 2. Who are God's elect? See Deuteronomy 7:6–8; Romans 9:6–23;

Ephesians 1:3–5; and 1 Peter 2:9. See also John 6:37–44, 15:16, 19; 1 Thessalonians 1:4–5; and James 2:5.

✦ 3. What is "the faith" of God's elect? What does it mean to have faith? See also John 6:29, 69 and Romans 10:17.

✦ 4. What is the link between "the faith" of God's elect and their "knowledge of the truth"? What is the faith of God's elect based on? See 1 Corinthians 15:1–6, 11.

✦ 5. What does it mean for "knowledge of the truth" to "[accord] with godliness"?

✦ 6. How does knowledge of the truth—knowledge of and belief in the gospel—lead to godly living?

✦ 7. Sum up in your own words Paul's apostolic purpose:

✦ 8. How does Paul's letter to Titus fit with his purpose?

♥ 9. Do you have faith and knowledge of the truth? Do you believe the gospel as Paul lays it out in 1 Corinthians 15:3–6?

♥ If not or if you are unsure, what questions do you have about the gospel message?

♥ If so, in what ways do your faith and knowledge accord with godliness in your life?

Day 3

Pray, then read Titus 1: 1–5.

Titus 1:2–3

👁 1. In what does Paul hope?

👁 2. Who has promised it, and when did he promise it?

👁 3. What does Paul write about God's character in verse 2?

✦ 4. How do God's character and the timing of the promise bolster Paul's hope?

✦ 5. How does Paul's hope motivate him to carry out his purpose?

👁 6. When was eternal life manifested, and what was it manifested in?

✦ 7. What is Paul referring to by "his word"? See 2 Timothy 1:10.

8. "Manifested" means revealed or showed. Through what does God reveal the hope of eternal life?

9. How do God's "word" and "the preaching" of Paul come together in verse 3 to reveal the hope of eternal life?

10. Who "entrusted" the preaching of the word to Paul?

11. What types of things are "entrusted" to others? What does this word tell us about the value of the message Paul is preaching?

12. Titus is well acquainted with Paul. He knows Paul is an apostle entrusted with the gospel. Why would Paul remind Titus of this here at the beginning of his letter? (Who else would read this letter? See Titus 3:15.)

13. How does one receive the "hope of eternal life"? See Titus 3:4–8.

✦14. What is this hope? Is it just living forever? See Titus 2:11–14.

✦15. Notice who promised and manifested the hope. Notice also who entrusted Paul with the message of this hope and commanded him to preach it. How does this give you confidence in Paul's message?

♥ 16. The hope of eternal life with Christ propels Paul in his ministry. In what way should that same hope propel us? How does the hope of eternal life motivate you?

♥ 17. How should this hope affect our faith and our knowledge of the truth?

Day 4

Pray, then read Titus 1:1–4.

Titus 1:4a

1. To whom does Paul write this letter?

2. How does Paul describe Titus?

3. Who was Titus, and why do you think Paul would call him his "true child"? See Titus 1:5ff; 2 Corinthians 8:23; and Galatians 2:1–3.

4. What does this familial term suggest about relationships in the church?

5. Why would Paul emphasize their "common faith"?

6. Titus was an uncircumcised Gentile. Paul was a Jew. In the first century, Jews would not even eat with unclean Gentiles. What does it say about the Christian faith that Paul would declare Titus to be his "true child in a common faith"?

♥ 7. Today most of us don't face a Jewish-Gentile divide. What are some of the divides you do see in your culture?

♥ 8. Based on Paul's relationship with Titus, how should these divides be handled in local churches?

♥ 9. What kinds of relationships do you have in your church? Do you have a child in the faith? A mother or father? True sisters and brothers? What can you do to cultivate deeper relationships?

♥ 10. Do you have relationships in your church with people who are different from you? Think about different national backgrounds but also different socioeconomic situations and different ages or stages of life. How can you cultivate relationships with people who are different from you?

Pray, then read Titus 1:1–4.

Titus 1:4b

👁 1. How does Paul greet Titus?

✦ 2. "Grace" means an undeserved gift. Jesus enabled "peace" with God through the sacrifice of his blood on the cross. Why does Paul greet the recipients of his letters with grace and peace from God?

✦ 3. Grace and peace come from God the Father and Christ Jesus. Why do you think Paul mentions both grace and peace together in his greeting? What point is he making with his readers?

✦ 4. Thirteen of Paul's letters are included in the Bible. In all of his other letters, Paul calls Jesus Lord. Why do you think he calls Jesus "our Savior" in this letter? (Paul also repeats "Savior," "salvation," and "saved" seven times in the letter.)

✦ 5. How does this letter itself impart grace and peace to its readers?

♥ 6. Take some time today to review what you've learned this week and pray for the Lord to build you up in the knowledge of the truth that leads to godliness as you study through Titus. Pray also for those who are studying with you.

Notes

Week 3

Pray this week for the elders of your church to be godly men who are above reproach, able to teach sound doctrine and willing to rebuke those who contradict sound doctrine.

Pray, then read Titus 1:1–16.

Titus 1:5

1. Where did Paul leave Titus?

2. What are the two tasks Paul left Titus to accomplish?

3. What does this imply about the churches on the island of Crete?

4. What do these two goals suggest about the organization of local churches?

5. Notice that "elders" is plural. Paul's pattern is to plant churches and appoint a plurality of elders to oversee those churches. See

Acts 14:23 and 2 Timothy 2:2. What does this tell you about the leadership of local churches today?

✛ 6. What is an "elder"? (The Bible also uses the terms "overseer" and "pastor" or "shepherd".) See Acts 20:17, 18; 1 Peter 5:1–3; and Hebrews 13:17.

✛ 7. Paul emphasizes his apostolic authority at the beginning of his letter to Titus in order to pass on that authority to Titus publicly. How would this letter help Titus in the tasks he is to carry out?

♥ 8. Why should women in the 21st century care about verse 5 and the description of elders that follows? Why is it important for women to know about the qualifications for elder office?

♥ 9. Do you know some of the elders of your church? How can you get to know them?

♥ 10. Take some time today to thank God for the elders of your church and pray for them.

Day 2

Pray, then read Titus 1:1–9.

Titus 1:6

👁 1. In the next verses, Paul reminds Titus what to look for in potential elders. What characteristics does he list in verse 6?

✦ 2. What does it mean to be "above reproach"?

✦ 3. Why would this be important for elders?

✦ 4. What does being "the husband of one wife" suggest?

✦ 5. Why would this be an important qualification for elders?

✦ 6. What does this statement assume about the gender of elders? See 1 Timothy 2:11–15 and 1 Corinthians 14:33–35.

✦ 7. Is Paul teaching that elders must be married and have multiple children? Or is he assuming that most men would be married with children and teaching the character of their leadership in the home? (Were the apostles all married? Did Jesus have a wife and children? Are there other instructions in Scripture about this?) Explain your answer.

✦ 8. The Greek word describing the children in verse 6 can be translated as "believers" or as "faithful." Looking at the whole of this verse do you think it is focused on the outward behavior or inward belief of a potential elder's children? Explain your answer:

✦ 9. Does a parent have control over whether a child becomes a believer? What should be expected of a Christian parent? See 1 Timothy 3:4–5. See also Ephesians 6:4. So what do you think is required for elders with regard to their children?

✦ 10. How would you summarize the expectation for elders in verse 6?

♥ 11. What do you learn from these expectations?

Day 3

Pray, then read Titus 1:5–16.

Titus 1:7

👁 1. "Overseer" is used interchangeably with "elder" in Titus and elsewhere in the Bible. (For example, 1 Peter 5:2.) What is an "overseer," and what must he be?

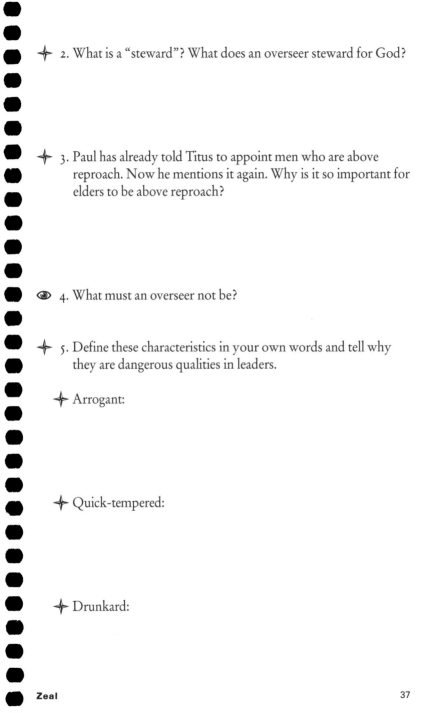

2. What is a "steward"? What does an overseer steward for God?

3. Paul has already told Titus to appoint men who are above reproach. Now he mentions it again. Why is it so important for elders to be above reproach?

4. What must an overseer not be?

5. Define these characteristics in your own words and tell why they are dangerous qualities in leaders.

Arrogant:

Quick-tempered:

Drunkard:

✦ Violent:

✦ Greedy for gain:

✦ 6. What do these things have in common?

♥ 7. Of course, it's not just leaders — no Christian should be characterized by these vices. Do you struggle with any of these? If so, how can you fight against them?

✦ 8. How are these characteristics related to being above reproach? If a leader in the church is arrogant, quick-tempered, a drunkard, violent, or greedy for gain, how does it reflect on Christ?

Pray, then read Titus 1:5–9.

Titus 1:8

👁 1. List the characteristics a man must have to be an overseer:

✦ 2. What does it mean to be "hospitable," and why would this virtue be important in an overseer?

✦ 3. What does it mean to be "a lover of good"? What would the opposite be? Why is this an important virtue for an overseer?

✦ 4. What does it mean to be "self-controlled"? What does "disciplined" mean? How would you distinguish these from one another, and why would they both be important for overseers?

✦ 5. How would you define being "upright" and "holy"? How would you distinguish these from one another? Why is it important for an overseer to be upright and holy?

✦ 6. What ties these characteristics together?

♥ 7. What is the world's general impression of people in authority in the church? How does this affect gospel outreach?

♥ 8. How is Jesus the perfect example of the characteristics in verses 7 and 8? And how can a man become more like Jesus?

✦ 9. Why is it so important for elders in the church to live this way and be above approach?

♥ 10. In which particular qualities listed in verse 8 would you like to grow? How can you cultivate these Christlike qualities in your life?

Day 5

Pray, then read Titus 1:5–16.

Titus 1:9

👁 1. To what must an elder hold firm?

👁 2. For what two reasons must he hold firm to the trustworthy word? (What are the duties of an elder?)

✦ 3. What is the "trustworthy word as taught," and why do you think Paul adds "as taught"? See 2 Timothy 2:2.

✦ 4. What does it mean to "hold firm to the trustworthy word as taught"?

✦ 5. What does it mean for doctrine to be "sound," and how is sound doctrine related to the "trustworthy word as taught"?

✦ 6. What is "instruction"?

✦ 7. What is "rebuke"?

✦ 8. Why are both of these needed in a local church?

✦ 9. How is verse 9 related to verses 7 and 8?

✦ 10. Elders are to be men who live out and teach sound doctrine. What does this tell us about the purpose of local churches?

How does the appointment of elders relate to Paul's purpose in verse 1?

♥ 11. What does it tell us about our needs as Christians?

♥ 12. What is your responsibility toward elders in your church? See also Hebrews 13:17–18.

Notes

Week 4

This week, pray for yourself and your church to be sound in the faith.

Pray, then read Titus 1:1–16.

Titus 1:10

✦ 1. Sum up verses 5–9 from last week:

👁 2. How does Paul describe the "many" of verse 10?

✦ 3. What does it mean to be "insubordinate"?

✦ 4. What is an "empty talker," and what is a "deceiver"?

✦ 5. Who are those of "the circumcision party"? See Acts 11:2–3;
      Galatians 2:11–14 and 5:2–6.

✦ 6. Why does Paul particularly name the circumcision party? What were they teaching, and why was it so dangerous? (See Acts 15:1.)

✦ 7. How does the "For" at the beginning of verse 10 connect the paragraphs?

♥ 8. Can you think of particular teachings today that are brought into the church by people who are insubordinate, empty talkers, and deceivers?

♥ 9. Are there any teachings today that you would compare to the teaching of the circumcision party?

♥ 10. What role do elders play in your life and the life of your church in guarding against false teaching?

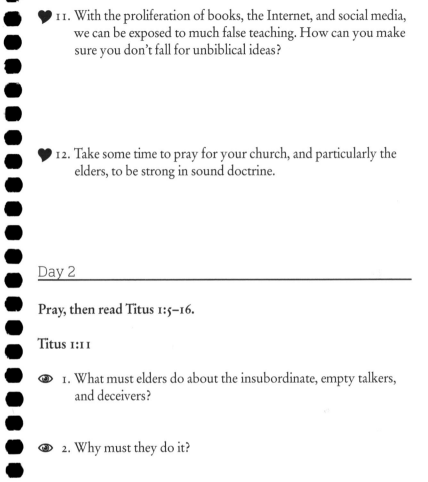

♥ 11. With the proliferation of books, the Internet, and social media, we can be exposed to much false teaching. How can you make sure you don't fall for unbiblical ideas?

♥ 12. Take some time to pray for your church, and particularly the elders, to be strong in sound doctrine.

Day 2

Pray, then read Titus 1:5–16.

Titus 1:11

👁 1. What must elders do about the insubordinate, empty talkers, and deceivers?

👁 2. Why must they do it?

👁 3. What is the motivation for these people to teach what ought not to be taught?

✦ 4. The Greek word for "upsetting" actually means overturning or ruining. What does this suggest is happening in the churches in Crete?

✦ 5. Look back at the characteristics of elders in verses 6–8. How do these characteristics protect the church and particularly equip these men to silence false teachers and help families who are misled?

♥ 6. If you hear false teaching by someone in your church, how should you handle it?

♥ 7. Does every theological mistake rise to the level of elders silencing the person? What is the difference between a member of the church holding a false view and someone trying to teach a false view? How would you handle these different circumstances?

Pray, then read Titus 1:9–16.

Titus 1:12–14

👁 1. What did a prophet of the Cretans say?

👁 2. What does Paul say about this testimony?

✦ 3. What kind of insight does this give us into the culture in which the Cretan Christians are living?

✦ 4. What kind of danger does this present to the faith of the Cretan Christians?

👁 5. Notice the "Therefore" in verse 13. What does Paul prescribe because of these tendencies among the Cretans?

👁 6. "Rebuke" is a negative term, and then Paul adds "sharply." But what is the goal of the rebuke?

✦ 7. Who is to be rebuked? (Who is the "them"? Who is the "they"?) Explain your answer:

♥ 8. Christians are supposed to be kind people who are unified. What do you think of Paul calling for sharp rebuke? Does this change your understanding of what it means to be loving? See 1 Timothy 1:3–5.

✦ 9. What does it mean to be "sound in the faith"? And how does the next clause further define "sound in the faith"?

♥ 10. Paul wants the Cretan church to be sound in the faith and to reject Jewish myths and the commands of people who reject the truth. We don't know exactly what these myths or commands were but they have to do with the circumcision party and are likely the same as described in 1 Timothy 1:4 and 4:1–5. What dangerous doctrines do local churches need to be wary of today?

♥ 11. Based on Titus 1:14, how would you write a statement, warning contemporary Christians about what to avoid?

Day 4

Pray, then read Titus 1:9–16.

Titus 1:15

◉ 1. What is pure to the pure?

◉ 2. What is pure to the defiled and unbelieving?

◉ 3. What is defiled in the defiled and unbelieving?

✦ 4. What does it mean to be "pure"?

✦ 5. What does it mean for one's mind and conscience to be "defiled"? See also 1 Timothy 6:3–5.

✦ 6. How is unbelief related to being defiled? See Romans 14:23b.

✦ 7. Jesus describes what defiles a person in Mark 7:14–23. Summarize his argument:

✦ 8. How does one become pure? See Titus 2:14.

✦ 9. Why does Paul insert this statement about purity and defilement here? What was the circumcision party likely telling the Cretan Christians?

✦ 10. Explain verse 15 in your own words:

♥ 11. In Mark 7, the religious leaders were complaining that Jesus' disciples did not do the ritual washing commanded by Jewish elders. (These were not commanded in Scripture.) What are some traditional rituals that Christians today might feel are necessary to please God?

♥ 12. If you were asked by a friend why you didn't engage in that ritual, how would you respond?

♥ 13. Are there any traditional rituals that you feel are helpful to you? How would you distinguish the way you practice these rituals from what the circumcision party was advocating?

♥ 14. Take some time to thank God for sending Jesus to bridge the gap between sinners and God and to rescue us from the tyranny of rituals. Because of his death we can be declared pure and can grow in purity until one day we see God face to face. See Matthew 5:8.

Day 5

Pray, then read Titus 1:5–2:1.

Titus 1:16

✦ 1. To whom does the "They" refer?

👁 2. What do they claim?

👁 3. How do they deny that claim?

👁 4. What are they?

✦ 5. What kinds of works deny God? See 1 John 2:3–6 and 9–11.

✦ 6. How does a person's works show what she really believes?

✦ 7. Why is it "detestable" for people to say they know God but deny him by the way they live?

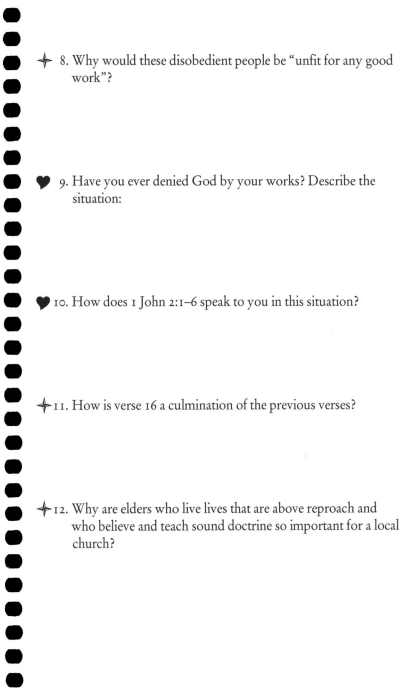

8. Why would these disobedient people be "unfit for any good work"?

9. Have you ever denied God by your works? Describe the situation:

10. How does 1 John 2:1–6 speak to you in this situation?

11. How is verse 16 a culmination of the previous verses?

12. Why are elders who live lives that are above reproach and who believe and teach sound doctrine so important for a local church?

♥ 13. What does a person's response to an elder's rebuke show about what she believes?

♥ 14. What are some of the traits that churches typically look for in elders or leaders?

♥ 15. Some churches have elders or leaders who are good men of high standing in the community but are not able to instruct in sound doctrine. Why is it dangerous to have a CEO-type model in mind for elders rather than choosing biblically qualified pastor-teachers?

♥ 16. Take some time to pray for your church. Pray for biblically qualified elders who are able to teach the congregation and to rebuke false teachers. Pray for the church to have soft hearts that respond well to sound teaching and to rebuke when needed.

Notes

Week 5

This week, pray to live a life that is increasingly consistent with the word of God.

Pray, then read Titus 1:15–2:10.

Titus 2:1–2

👁 1. What is Titus to do?

✦ 2. What contrast does Paul set up by using the word "but"?

✦ 3. Titus 1:1 refers to "knowledge of the truth, which accords with godliness." Knowing sound doctrine leads to living godly lives. What is Titus being told to teach in 2:1? What accords with sound doctrine?

✦ 4. How do verses 2–10 relate to verse 1?

♥ 5. To whom would this command apply today?

👁 6. What traits are older men in the church to have?

✦ 7. Explain each of these traits:

   ✦ Sober-minded

   ✦ Dignified

   ✦ Self-controlled

   ✦ Sound in faith

   ✦ Sound in love

Zeal

✦ Sound in steadfastness

✦ 8. From what you know about Cretan culture, would these traits have been typical for older men? What would have stood out as different?

✦ 9. How would these traits contrast with those of the false teachers in 1:10–16?

✦ 10. How do these characteristics accord with sound doctrine (the gospel)?

♥ 11. What about today? In what ways would a man with these characteristics stand out?

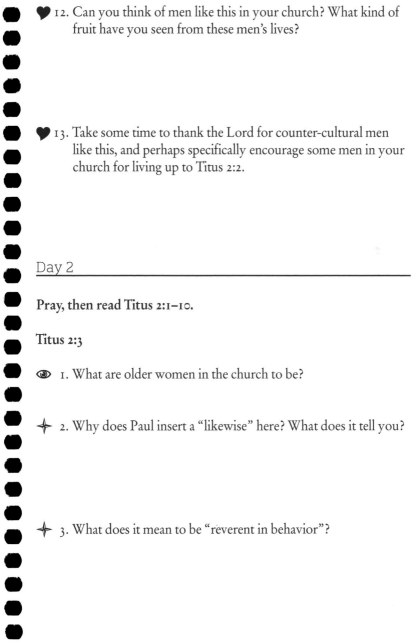

12. Can you think of men like this in your church? What kind of fruit have you seen from these men's lives?

13. Take some time to thank the Lord for counter-cultural men like this, and perhaps specifically encourage some men in your church for living up to Titus 2:2.

Day 2

Pray, then read Titus 2:1–10.

Titus 2:3

1. What are older women in the church to be?

2. Why does Paul insert a "likewise" here? What does it tell you?

3. What does it mean to be "reverent in behavior"?

♥ 4. What would it look like for a woman to be irreverent?

✦ 5. What is a "slanderer"?

♥ 6. How does slander affect the church?

✦ 7. What does it mean for a woman to be a "slave to much wine"?

♥ 8. What kind of effect does excessive drinking have on a person's behavior and tongue?

✦ 9. Why is it important for Christian women to be reverent and not engage in slander or drunkenness? Why do you think Paul would emphasize these particular things?

♥ 10. Do you struggle with any of these behaviors? Considering Titus 1:1–2, what can you do to fight against them?

♥ 11. How can your sisters in the church help you resist these behaviors?

Day 3

Pray, then read Titus 2:1–10.

Titus 2:3–4

👁 1. What are older women to teach?

👁 2. What are they to train the young women to do?

✦ 3. How do you think Paul would define an "older woman," and what is a "young" woman?

✦ 4. Why does Paul instruct Titus to have older women teach and train younger women? He doesn't have the same instructions for older men.

✦ 5. Look at the list in verses 4–5. What is the focus of the things on the list?

✦ 6. Are these things particular behaviors or are they character traits?

✦ 7. Define each of the traits and describe what the opposite character trait would look like:

✦ Love their husbands and children

✦ Self-controlled

✦ Pure

✦ Working at home

✦ Kind

✦ Submissive to their own husband

♥ 8. Why would young women need to be trained to love their husbands and children? What might they love instead?

♥ 9. What might result from loving something else more?

♥ 10. What would training a woman to love her husband and children look like?

♥ 11. Why is it important for young women to be trained in self-control and purity? Why might these be particularly important in today's culture?

♥ 12. How are you doing in the areas of self-control and purity? How might you seek help in these areas from an older woman in your church?

✦ 13. Read Proverbs 31:16, 18 and 24. Considering Proverbs 31 and also the focus of verses 4–5 on character traits (as opposed to specific behaviors), do you think the phrase "working at home": a) prohibits women from working outside the home, or b) means they should be busy at home instead of lazy? Explain your answer:

♥ 14. In what ways are you tempted to be lazy at home? What encourages you to work hard?

♥ 15. How are you doing in the area of kindness? See also Proverbs 31:26.

♥ 16. How can an older woman in the church help a young woman to learn to work in the home and be kind?

♥ 17. Take some time today to pray that these traits would be increasing in your life.

Pray, then read Titus 2:1–10.

Titus 2:5

👁 1. What is the last trait that Paul lists in verse 5?

✦ 2. What does it mean for a wife to be "submissive to" her husband? See Ephesians 5:22–24, 33 and 1 Peter 3:1–6.

✦ 3. Is submissiveness a particular set of behaviors? Is it a personality type? Is it an attitude? Explain your answer:

✦ 4. Does submission mean that women are unequal or inferior to men or that a wife is inferior to her husband? See Genesis 1:27; 1 Corinthians 11:11–12; Galatians 3:28 and 1 Peter 3:7. Explain your answer:

✦ 5. Does submission only apply to wives of believing husbands? See 1 Peter 3:1–2.

♥ 6. What does the world think of submission? How would you explain the goodness of biblical submission?

♥ 7. Explain why biblical submission does not include the following, and describe how a wife could have an appropriately submissive attitude in the situation:

♥ Never disagreeing with your husband

♥ Engaging in sin because your husband asks you to

♥ Allowing abuse

♥ Allowing adultery or pornography

♥ 8. What are some areas in which you struggle to submit to your husband? Consider your finances, parenting, the way you speak, intimacy, time, etc.

♥ 9. How does your response to your husband in these areas affect your relationship with your husband and the atmosphere in your home? How does it affect your relationship with God?

♥ 10. How can we women in the church help each other to be submissive wives?

♥ 11. If you are not yet married but desire to be, how does the command to wives to submit to their husbands affect your consideration of what type of man to marry?

♥ 12. How can those of us who are older help young women who aren't yet married prepare to be submissive wives?

Pray, then read Titus 1:16–2:15.

Titus 2:5

✦ 1. Examining the list in verses 4–5, what would you say is the priority of a married woman?

◉ 2. Why are these character traits so important?

✦ 3. How does "sound doctrine" (v. 1) accord with these characteristics?

✦ 4. How might the word of God have been reviled if Christian women in Crete did not behave consistently with these character traits?

♥ 5. How might the word of God be reviled today if we in the church do not behave consistently with these character traits?

♥ 6. Do you have or have you had an "older woman" in your life who is teaching you? Describe your relationship. If you don't have an older woman in your life, is there someone in your church who might be able to fill that role? How could you approach her about this?

♥ 7. Do you have a "young" woman in your life? How are you intentionally teaching her what is good, and so training her? If there is not a young woman in your life, who might benefit from your teaching? How could you approach her about this?

♥ 8. In first-century Crete, women almost universally would have lived with their parents until marriage. Singleness would have been rare. How is our culture today different, and how does that difference impact our application of verses 4 and 5?

♥ 9. Which of the character traits listed in verses 4–5 do you struggle with most? Whether you are single or married, how can you work on those traits? (Consider the overarching truth that Paul teaches in Titus that sound doctrine leads to godliness.)

♥ 10. Do you think about behaviors that might cause the word of God to be reviled? Are you motivated to avoid them for the glory of God's name? Explain:

Notes

This week, pray for you and your brothers and sisters in the church to live lives that adorn the doctrine of God our Savior.

Pray, then read Titus 1:16–2:15.

Titus 2:6–7

👁 1. Reminder: what does Paul tell Timothy to teach in verse 1?

👁 2. What is Titus to urge the younger men?

✦ 3. Why does he start the sentence with "likewise"?

✦ 4. There was an extensive list of things for older women to teach young women. Why does Paul want Titus to focus on self-control for younger men?

✦ 5. Notice that "self-control" is a character trait listed for both men and women, young and old. What is self-control?

✦ 6. Why do you think this was such an important trait to teach and model, particularly in Crete?

♥ 7. Why is self-control important today? What happens in a church if the members lack self-control?

👁 8. What is Titus to "show [himself]… to be"?

✦ 9. What might it look like for Titus, the pastor, to "model… good works"?

✦ 10. How is Titus' modeling of good works connected to his teaching of the younger men?

♥ 11. What happens in a church where the pastor is "a model of good works"? What happens if he is not? Have you seen examples of either of these?

Pray, then read Titus 2:1–10.

Titus 2:7–8

👁 1. What is Titus to show in his teaching?

👁 2. Why is Titus to be "a model of good works" and show "integrity, dignity, and sound speech" in his teaching?

✦ 3. What is "integrity" and how would it show in teaching? See 2 Corinthians 4:1–2.

✦ 4. What is "dignity" and how would it show in teaching? See 2 Timothy 4:2.

✦ 5. What is "sound speech that cannot be condemned," and how would it show in teaching? See 2 Timothy 4:2–5.

✦ 6. Titus is to be "a model of good works." How might a lack of good works or some kind of immorality give an "opponent" evil things to say about Titus?

✦ 7. How might a lack of integrity or dignity in his teaching give opponents evil things to say about Titus?

✦ 8. How might a lack of unsound speech in his teaching give opponents evil things to say about Titus?

✦ 9. Why would an opponent be put to shame by Titus showing good works and teaching with integrity, dignity, and sound speech?

✦ 10. To whom does the "us" at the end of verse 8 refer?

♥ 11. Who looks bad today when a pastor is immoral or lacks integrity, dignity, or sound speech? Explain your answer:

♥ 12. Do you have anyone who looks to you as a model, or do you teach anyone? What do verses 7–8 have to say to you about your life and speech?

Day 3

Pray, then read Titus 1:16–2:1–15.

Titus 2:9–10

👁 1. What are bondservants to be?

👁 2. What are bondservants not to be?

👁 3. What are they to show?

👁 4. Why are they to behave in this way?

✦ 5. What does it mean for "bondservants… to be submissive"? How does the second phrase in the sentence (after the semi-colon and before the "so that") help define the first?

✦ 6. Bond-service was a common economic arrangement in the first-century Greco-Roman world and was not like the reprehensible practice of race-based chattel slavery of 17th- and 18th-Century America. Along with other differences, bondservants could earn money and buy back their freedom. Even so, the apostle Paul tells bondservants to gain their freedom if they can (1 Corinthians 7:21) and tells a slave owner to accept his slave back as no longer a slave but as a brother (Philemon 16–17). To whom would verses 9–10 apply today?

✦ 7. What does it mean to "adorn the doctrine of God our Savior"? What is this doctrine and what does it mean for it to be adorned?

✦ 8. How can a bondservant's submissive behavior "adorn the doctrine of God our Savior"?

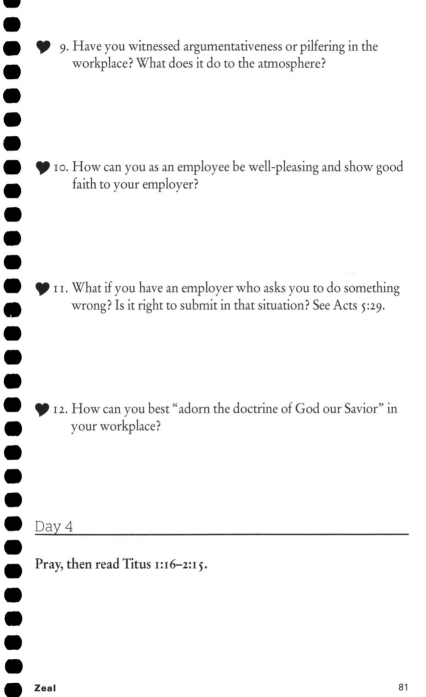

9. Have you witnessed argumentativeness or pilfering in the workplace? What does it do to the atmosphere?

10. How can you as an employee be well-pleasing and show good faith to your employer?

11. What if you have an employer who asks you to do something wrong? Is it right to submit in that situation? See Acts 5:29.

12. How can you best "adorn the doctrine of God our Savior" in your workplace?

Day 4

Pray, then read Titus 1:16–2:15.

Titus 2:1–10

◉ 1. Paul's instructions to Titus cover everyone in the church: older men and women, young men and women, and slaves. What does verse 1 tell us is the basis for all the teaching Titus is to do?

◉ 2. Find everywhere Paul writes "that" or "so that" in verses 2–10. Write down the phrases that follow those words:

✦ 3. What do the "that's" or "so that's" tell us about these phrases? How are the phrases connected to the teaching instructions?

✦ 4. What is the ultimate result of living in accord with sound doctrine?

✦ 5. How does this result motivate Christian living?

✦ 6. What do you think of Paul's concern with the way outsiders perceive Christians? Why do you think he emphasizes making doctrine look good by the way we live our lives?

♥ 7. Have you ever witnessed Christians behave in ways or have attitudes that caused the word of God to be reviled? Describe:

♥ 8. Have you witnessed Christians in your church who have adorned "the doctrine of God our Savior"? Describe:

♥ 9. What are you motivated to do by the "that" and "so that" phrases?

Day 5

Pray, then read Titus 1:16–2:15.

♥ 1. In chapter 2, Paul is telling Titus to instruct the church in godly behavior. In fact, Paul's entire letter to Titus emphasizes good works. Is it okay for a pastor to set aside doctrine and merely teach good behavior? Why or why not?

2. Why is the "knowledge of the truth" important to living godly lives?

3. After studying verses 1–10, are there any attitudes or behaviors that you would like to change to protect the reputation of the word of God?

4. Are there any attitudes or behaviors you would like to grow in to better adorn the doctrine of Christ?

5. How will you use the Scriptures and prayer to change and grow?

♥ 6. How will you use the church?

Notes

Week 7

Give God praise this week for sending his Son, Jesus, to redeem and purify a people for himself. Pray to eagerly await the return of "our great God and Savior Jesus Christ."

Pray, then read Titus 2:1–15.

Titus 2:11

✦ 1. Verse 11 begins with "For." How are verses 11–15 connected with the previous verses?

◉ 2. What has "appeared"?

◉ 3. What is it (or he) bringing and for whom?

✦ 4. To what (or to whom) does "the grace of God" refer?

✦ 5. Why would Paul use the phrase "the grace of God" here?

✦ 6. What does it mean that "the grace of God has appeared"?

✦ 7. What does "salvation" mean? What are people saved from, and what are they saved for? See Romans 8:1–4.

✦ 8. How is it that the grace of God brings salvation?

✦ 9. How does Titus 1:2–3 relate to the grace of God appearing, bringing salvation?

✦ 10. In what sense is salvation "for all people"? How does this relate to verses 1–10, and how does this have an equalizing effect?

♥ 11. Have you repented of your sins and believed on Jesus and been saved? If so, how has this changed your life? If not, why not?

♥ 12. How should the fact that "the grace of God has appeared, bringing salvation for all people" affect our evangelism?

♥ 13. Stop and reflect on verse 11: "For the grace of God has appeared, bringing salvation for all people." What is your response to this glorious news?

Day 2

Pray, then read Titus 2:1–15.

Titus 2:12

👁 1. In addition to bringing salvation, what else has the grace of God done?

✦ 2. What is "ungodliness"? See 1:7, 10, 12, 16 and 2:14. See also James 4:4.

✦ 3. What are "worldly passions"? See 3:3. See also James 3:16 and 4:1–2.

✦ 4. What does it mean "to live self-controlled, upright, and godly lives"? How does this correspond with what we studied last week in 2:1–10?

✦ 5. How does the grace of God train us "to renounce ungodliness and worldly passions, and to live self-controlled, upright, and godly lives"?

✦ 6. Why or how would the gospel of Christ lead to self-control?

Week 7

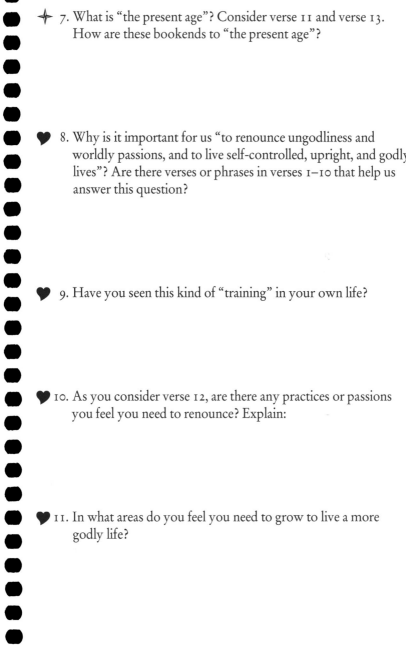

7. What is "the present age"? Consider verse 11 and verse 13. How are these bookends to "the present age"?

8. Why is it important for us "to renounce ungodliness and worldly passions, and to live self-controlled, upright, and godly lives"? Are there verses or phrases in verses 1–10 that help us answer this question?

9. Have you seen this kind of "training" in your own life?

10. As you consider verse 12, are there any practices or passions you feel you need to renounce? Explain:

11. In what areas do you feel you need to grow to live a more godly life?

♥ 12. How, specifically, can the grace of God train you for these things?

Day 3

Pray, then read Titus 2:1–15.

Titus 2:13

👁 1. What are we waiting for?

👁 2. What is our "blessed hope"?

✦ 3. What does "blessed hope" mean? See also 1:2.

👁 4. How is Jesus described in verse 13?

✦ 5. What does this description tell us about who Jesus is, and how does that relate to our blessed hope?

✦ 6. Verse 11 tells us that "the grace of God **has appeared,** bringing salvation," but verse 13 tells us that we are **"waiting"** for the appearing of our "Savior Jesus Christ." How is it that he has appeared but we are waiting for him to appear?

✦ 7. How will Jesus' second appearing be different from the first, and what does the word "glory" in verse 13 have to do with it? See also 1 Thessalonians 1:7–10.

♥ 8. What does "waiting" have to do with how we live our lives? See Acts 1:6–11, 2 Peter 3:11–14 and 1 John 3:2–3.

♥ 9. How does "our blessed hope" motivate you to live a godly life in this present age?

♥ 10. Do you think of yourself as living life, eagerly awaiting Christ's return? If so, how does it affect the way you live? If not, how would your life change if you did?

♥ 11. How can you keep "the appearing of our great God and Savior Jesus Christ" more at the forefront of your mind and life?

Day 4

Pray, then read Titus 2:10b–15.

Titus 2:14

👁 1. What did Jesus Christ do?

👁 2. Why did he do it?

👁 3. What should God's people be?

✦ 4. How did Christ give himself? See Matthew 20:28 and Philippians 2:6–8.

✦ 5. What does "redeem us from all lawlessness" mean? See 1 Corinthians 6:20 and 1 Peter 1:18.

✦ 6. Why must God's people be purified? See also Ezekiel 37:23.

✦ 7. What does it mean to be "a people for [God's] own possession?" See Deuteronomy 7:6–8. See also Deuteronomy 26:18–19; Exodus 19:4–6; and Malachi 3:17–18.

✦ 8. In the passages listed in question 7, how is holiness connected to being God's "treasured possession"?

✦ 9. Who are the people Christ redeemed to be set apart for God's treasured possession? Explain your answer. See 1 Peter 2:9–10. (Read through verse 12 to see the same connection to holiness we saw in the Old Testament passages.)

✦ 10. What does it mean to be "zealous for good works"?

✦ 11. How are "good works" and godliness rooted in Jesus' death?

✦ 12. How are they rewarded by the appearing of his glory?

♥ 13. If you have put your trust in our great God and Savior Jesus Christ, he has redeemed you "from all lawlessness." What does that mean to you personally?

♥ 14. Are you "zealous for good works"? What good works are you engaged in and what motivates you to do these good works?

Day 5

Pray, then read Titus 1:16–2:15.

Titus 2:15

👁 1. What three things does Paul tell Titus to do?

2. What are the "things" Titus is to declare?

3. What does it mean to "exhort"?

4. What does it mean to "rebuke with all authority"? What authority does Titus have?

5. What is Titus to let no one do?

6. Why do you think Paul is emphasizing Titus' authority to teach here? Does it have anything to do with the first chapter? Why is it important that no one disregards Titus?

7. How do elders in local churches exercise this authority today? From where do they derive their authority?

♥ 8. Why is it so important for elders today to "Declare these things; exhort and rebuke"?

♥ 9. What is your attitude toward authority in the church? Are you eager to listen to teaching? Do you assess it according to God's word? Do you respond by doing what you are exhorted to do? How do you respond to rebuke in a sermon or personal conversation?

♥ 10. What are some ways you can encourage your elders in their work of declaring, exhorting, and rebuking? See also Hebrews 13:17.

Notes

Week 8

This week, give God praise for his mercy in Christ Jesus and pray to be gentle, obedient, and ready for every good work.

Pray, then read Titus 2:11–3:10.

Titus 3:1–2

✦ 1. To whom does "them" refer?

✦ 2. In verses 1–2, is Paul addressing how the church is to treat one another or how they are to behave toward outsiders? Explain your answer:

👁 3. From verses 1–2, list the things Paul tells Titus to remind the church:

✦ 4. What "rulers and authorities" is Paul writing about, and what does it mean to be "submissive" to them?

✦ 5. How does "be obedient" add to being "submissive"?

✦ 6. What does it mean to "be ready for every good work"?

✦ 7. Why is it important for Christians "to be submissive to rulers and authorities, to be obedient, to be ready for every good work"?

✦ 8. How are the commands of verse 2 related to one another?

✦ 9. Why is it important for Christians to obey the commands of verse 2?

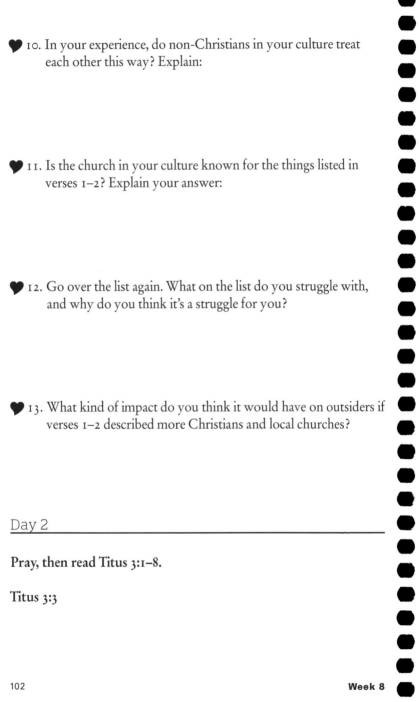

♥ 10. In your experience, do non-Christians in your culture treat each other this way? Explain:

♥ 11. Is the church in your culture known for the things listed in verses 1–2? Explain your answer:

♥ 12. Go over the list again. What on the list do you struggle with, and why do you think it's a struggle for you?

♥ 13. What kind of impact do you think it would have on outsiders if verses 1–2 described more Christians and local churches?

Day 2

Pray, then read Titus 3:1–8.

Titus 3:3

👁 1. What were "we ourselves"?

✦ 2. Verse 3 starts with the word "For." What is the For there for? How is verse 3 connected to verses 1–2?

✦ 3. In what circumstances would a Christian be tempted to disobey, speak evil, quarrel, or be unkind and discourteous?

✦ 4. How does recognizing that we were once just like the world around us help us to be verse 1 and 2 people?

♥ 5. If you are a Christian, how does verse 3 make you feel when you meditate on it and think about your previous state?

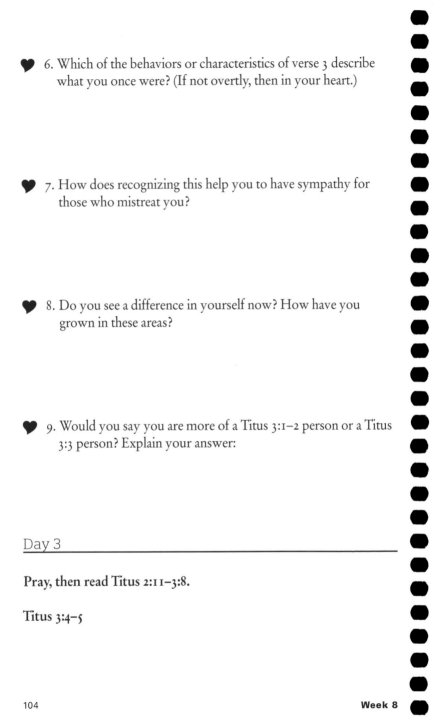

♥ 6. Which of the behaviors or characteristics of verse 3 describe what you once were? (If not overtly, then in your heart.)

♥ 7. How does recognizing this help you to have sympathy for those who mistreat you?

♥ 8. Do you see a difference in yourself now? How have you grown in these areas?

♥ 9. Would you say you are more of a Titus 3:1–2 person or a Titus 3:3 person? Explain your answer:

Day 3

Pray, then read Titus 2:11–3:8.

Titus 3:4–5

Week 8

1. What does the "But" in verse 4 signal? How do verses 4 and following relate to verse 3?

2. What happened and when?

3. What is "the goodness and loving kindness of God our Savior"? How has God been good and shown his loving kindness? Compare 2:11.

4. To whom does the "he" in verse 5 refer?

5. What did not save us?

6. "According to" what did he save us?

7. "By" what did he save us?

8. Did God save us because of something we did? Why would Paul use the word "mercy" here, and what does it have to do with verse 3?

+ 9. What is "the washing of regeneration and renewal of the Holy Spirit"? See Ezekiel 36:25–29; John 3:3–8 and 1 Corinthians 6:9–11. What does this have to do with salvation? And how does renewal follow from regeneration?

+ 10. What is the outward symbol for this washing that God has given to the church?

+ 11. How do verses 4–5 deliver us from verse 3 and enable us for verses 1–2?

♥ 12. If you are a Christian, you were once a verse 3 person. What is your response to being mercifully delivered from a verse 3 life?

♥ 13. How does God's mercy, goodness, and loving kindness toward you motivate you to treat unbelievers with mercy, goodness, and loving kindness?

Pray, then read Titus 3:1–8.

Titus 3:6–7

👁 1. What has God done with the Holy Spirit and through whom has he done it?

👁 2. Which word tells you that God does not hold back when he pours out the Holy Spirit?

✦ 3. According to verse 4–6, which persons of the Trinity are involved in saving sinners?

✦ 4. What does Jesus Christ our Savior have to do with the Holy Spirit being poured out? See John 16:7–11 and Acts 2:32–33.

👁 5. Why did God pour out his Holy Spirit on us?

✦ 6. What does "being justified by his grace" mean? See 2:14.

✦ 7. What is an "heir" and to whom are we heirs?

✦ 8. What does "heirs according to the hope of eternal life" mean? What does this have to do with the Holy Spirit? See also 1:2; 2 Corinthians 1:21–22; and Ephesians 1:13–14.

✦ 9. How does verse 7 speak to both our present state and our future?

♥ 10. What does it mean for you that God has given himself richly to you by the Holy Spirit? See also Romans 5:5.

♥ 11. What does it mean for your life that you, as an "heir," have the Holy Spirit dwelling in you as a downpayment, guaranteeing "eternal life"?

Week 8

Pray, then read Titus 2:11–3:11.

✦ 1. What parallels can you find between 2:11–14 and 3:1–8?

✦ 2. Why do you think Paul inserts the gospel in both of these sections of his letter?

✦ 3. Why does Paul in these two sections specifically remind Titus and the church of the hope they have?

♥ 4. What kinds of changes should be evident in someone on whom the Holy Spirit has been poured out?

♥ 5. How should the Holy Spirit's work make local churches look different from the surrounding culture?

Notes

Week 9

Pray for yourself and the other members of your local church to be devoted to good works as a result of their commitment to sound doctrine.

Pray, then read Titus 3.

Titus 3:8

✦ 1. What "saying is trustworthy"?

◉ 2. What does Paul instruct Titus to do?

✦ 3. What "things" is Paul referring to?

◉ 4. Why is Titus to "insist on these things"?

✦ 5. What basis do you see in verse 8 for devoting oneself to good works? Or what kind of people "devote themselves to good works"?

👁 6. How does Paul describe "good works"?

✦ 7. How is doing the good works described in Titus "excellent and profitable"?

♥ 8. How have you seen the good works of people in your church be excellent and profitable?

♥ 9. In your experience, has doing good works been excellent and profitable for you, or is it difficult to "renounce ungodliness and worldly passions" and live a godly life?

♥ 10. Would you describe yourself as being devoted to good works? How would you like to improve in this area?

Day 2

Pray, then read Titus 2:15–3:11.

Titus 3:9–11

✦ 1. What contrast is signaled by the word "But" in verse 9?

◉ 2. What is Titus to "avoid"?

◉ 3. Why is he to avoid these controversies?

✦ 4. How does Paul contrast Titus spending time on instructing the church on good works with spending time on foolish controversies? Notice the contrasting words at the end of verse 8 and the end of verse 9.

◉ 5. What is Titus to do about a person who "stirs up division"?

◉ 6. What is Titus to "know" about this person?

◉ 7. What is this person?

✦ 8. Paul doesn't give the specifics of what "genealogies, dissensions, and quarrels about the law" were, but they are all "foolish

controversies." How would you define foolish controversies?
See 1:10–16.

✦ 9. In verse 2, Paul has instructed the church "to show perfect
courtesy toward all people." But in verse 10, he instructs the
church to "have nothing more to do with" a person? What
is the difference between the verse 2 person and the verse 10
person?

✦ 10. What does it mean for Titus and the church to "have nothing
more to do with" a person?

✦ 11. How is this divisive person "warped," "sinful," and "self-
condemned"?

♥ 12. What do these verses tell us about the importance of unity in
the local church?

♥ 13. What do these verses imply about what we should be focused on in the church?

✦ 14. In verse 10, Paul is telling Titus to exercise church discipline. Read also Matthew 18:15–17 and 1 Corinthians 5:1–5. Describe the process of church discipline:

✦ 15. What is the purpose of church discipline?

♥ 16. Why is church discipline necessary for a local church's unity and health?

♥ 17. Paul starts his letter to Titus highlighting the importance of "knowledge of the truth" (1:1) and roots all of his instruction in doctrine (2:11–14 and 3:3–7). He writes that elders must "be able to give instruction in sound doctrine and also rebuke those who contradict it" (1:9) and tells Titus to "teach what accords with sound doctrine" (2:1). Some today say that doctrine is inherently divisive; yet Paul advocates teaching and believing sound doctrine and rebuking those who don't, while warning against divisiveness (1:11 and 3:9–11). How would you explain this?

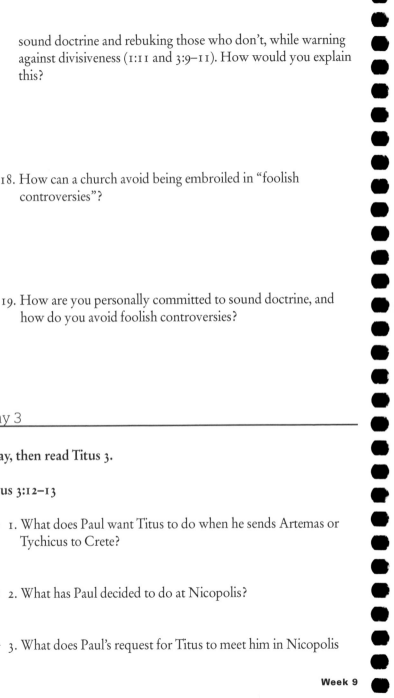 18. How can a church avoid being embroiled in "foolish controversies"?

19. How are you personally committed to sound doctrine, and how do you avoid foolish controversies?

Day 3

Pray, then read Titus 3.

Titus 3:12–13

1. What does Paul want Titus to do when he sends Artemas or Tychicus to Crete?

2. What has Paul decided to do at Nicopolis?

3. What does Paul's request for Titus to meet him in Nicopolis

tell you about Titus' role in Crete and the importance of his teaching and appointing elders?

4. What are Paul's instructions with regard to Zenas and Apollos?

5. Who do you suppose Artemas and Tychicus were? How would they have been connected to Paul? (Artemas is not mentioned elsewhere in the Bible. Tychicus is mentioned several times, including Colossians 4:7–8.)

6. Who are Zenas and Apollos, and why do you think Paul wants them to be sped on their way, lacking nothing? (Zenos is not mentioned elsewhere in the Bible. Apollos is mentioned several times, including Acts 18:24–28.)

7. What do these verses tell you about Paul's ministry and relationships?

♥ 8. How does your church care for and support missionaries? How do you participate in this care and support?

Day 4

Pray, then read Titus 3.

Titus 3:14–15.

✦ 1. To whom does the "our people" refer?

✦ 2. What does the "our" tell you about how Paul identifies with the church?

👁 3. What does Paul want the church to "learn"?

👁 4. Why does he want them to "devote themselves to good works"?

✦ 5. How would the church continue to learn this? How is verse 14 related to the rest of Titus?

✦ 6. Why would the church "be unfruitful" if they were not devoting themselves to good works?

✦ 7. What does verse 14 tell you about the kind of community a church should be?

♥ 8. How has your church helped those in "urgent need"? How have you been a part of this?

♥ 9. Notice that Paul instructs believers to "devote themselves to good works" in both verse 8 and verse 14. How can you personally continue to learn to devote yourself to good works?

Zeal

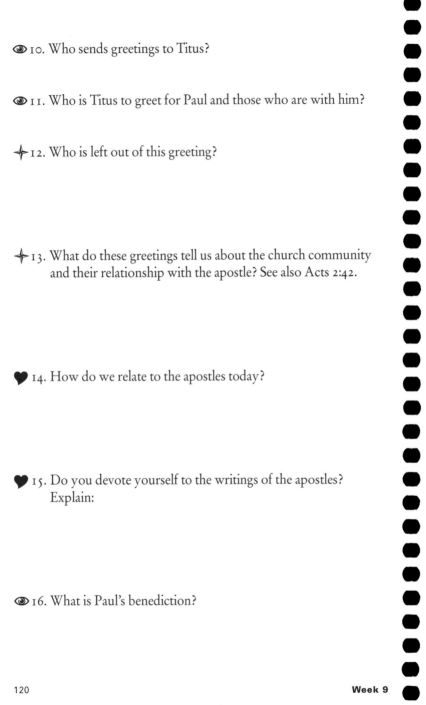

10. Who sends greetings to Titus?

11. Who is Titus to greet for Paul and those who are with him?

12. Who is left out of this greeting?

13. What do these greetings tell us about the church community and their relationship with the apostle? See also Acts 2:42.

14. How do we relate to the apostles today?

15. Do you devote yourself to the writings of the apostles? Explain:

16. What is Paul's benediction?

✦17. What does this benediction convey?

✦18. Notice the "all" in the benediction. What does this tell you about whom Paul expected to read this letter?

Day 5

Pray, then read through Titus.

✦ 1. Why did Paul write this letter to Titus?

✦ 2. If someone asked you what the book of Titus was about, how would you sum it up?

✦ 3. How would you explain the importance of sound doctrine and its relationship to godliness and good works?

✦ 4. What does Titus teach us about the organization, leadership, and focus of a local church?

✦ 5. How does Titus teach churches to deal with false doctrine?

♥ 6. What have you learned from the book of Titus? What stood out to you?

♥ 7. What have you read in Titus that convicted your heart?

♥ 8. How has your life changed as a result of studying Titus?

Notes

Inductive Bible Studies for Women by Keri Folmar

Endorsed by Kathleen Nielson, Diane Schreiner,
Connie Dever, Kristie Anyabwile, Gloria Furman

JOY! – A Bible Study
on Philippians
for Women
A 10-week study

GRACE: A Bible
Study on Ephesians
for Women
A 10-week study

FAITH: A Bible
Study on James
for Women
A 10-week study

A Bible Study for Women on the Gospel of Mark

SON OF GOD
Volume 1
An 11-week study

SON OF GOD
Volume 2
An 11-week study

"It is hard to imagine a better inductive Bible Study tool."
–Diane Schreiner

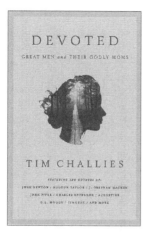

Devoted
Great Men and Their Godly Moms

by Tim Challies | 126 pages

Christian mothers shaped the men who changed the world.

Featuring the mothers of John Newton, Hudson Taylor, J. Gresham Machen, John Piper, Charles Spurgeon, Augustine, D.L. Moody, Timothy, and more.

bit.ly/devotedbook

"*Devoted* offers rich encouragement, wisdom, and hope for any mom who longs for her sons and daughters to follow, love, and serve Christ."

Nancy DeMoss Wolgemuth, author, teacher, and host of Revive Our Hearts

"*Devoted* will encourage moms (and dads) in the trenches, but also pour out grace and hope on the parents of prodigals. Reading this book was sheer delight and I highly recommend it."

Kimberly Wagner, author, Fierce Women

"Tim has collected for us the stories of women whose greatness was largely hidden. The devoted lives of these eleven women will inspire and encourage you. Their stories and examples, so easily overlooked, are now presented in this accessible and helpful book."

Trillia Newbell, author, God's Very Good Idea, and Enjoy

"Challies describes the powerful influence of a godly mother in articulate detail through stories of real women who have gone before us. These women believe the same gospel and cling to the same Christ, and I pray this book encourages many more mothers to follow their lead."

Gloria Furman, author, Missional Motherhood

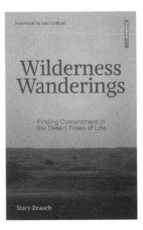

Wilderness Wanderings
Finding Contentment in the Desert Times of Life

by Stacy Reaoch
Foreword by Jani Ortlund

25 devotionals for women reflecting on our journey to the Promised Land

120 pages
bit.ly/wilwand

"I found myself encouraged and challenged by the biblical, insightful, and practical wisdom woven throughout."
>   *Sarah Walton, co-author of Hope When It Hurts – Biblical Reflections to Help You Grasp God's Purpose in Your Suffering*

"We highly recommend this book for careful, prayerful reflection."
>   *Bruce and Jodi Ware, Southern Seminary*

"Consider this delightful devotional your must-have guide for any season of wandering."
>   *Erin Davis, author and blogger*

"Stacy Reaoch is a gifted guide for real joy in hard places."
>   *David Mathis, executive editor, desiringGod.org; pastor; author*

"A tonic for the soul....biblically faithful, spiritually challenging, and encouraging. A wonderful resource for both personal reading and for group discussion."
>   *Tom and Diane Schreiner, Southern Seminary*

"A guidebook through these barren and difficult paths, and a drink of cool water for the weary traveler."
>   *Megan Hill, author; editorial board member, Christianity Today*

Happily Ever After
Finding Grace in the Messes of Marriage

by John Piper, Francis Chan, Nancy DeMoss Wolgemuth, and 10 more

Marriage...Harder than you expected, better than a fairy tale.

bit.ly/DG-HAPPILY

PARTIAL TABLE OF CONTENTS

The Scars That Have Shaped Me
How God Meets Us in Suffering

by Vaneethat Rendall Risner
Foreword by Joni Eareckson Tada

"Raw, transparent, terrifiying, and yet amazingly hopeful!"
Brian Fikkert, co-author of *When Helping Hurts*

bit.ly/THESCARS

"Vaneetha writes with creativity, biblical faithfulness, compelling style, and an experiential authenticity that draws other sufferers in. Here you will find both a tested life and a love for the sovereignty of a good and gracious God."

*John Piper, author of **Desiring God** and many other books*

"*The Scars That Have Shaped Me* will make you weep and rejoice not just because it brims with authenticity and integrity, but because every page points you to the rest that is found in entrusting your life to one who is in complete control and is righteous, powerful, wise, and good in every way."

Paul Tripp, pastor, author, international conference speaker

""I could not put this book down, except to wipe my tears. Vaneetha's testimony of God's kindness to her in pain was exactly what I needed; no doubt, many others will feel the same. It has helped me process my own grief and loss, and given me renewed hope to care for those in my life who suffer in various ways."

*Gloria Furman, author, **Missional Motherhood; Alive in Him***

"Vaneetha Risner's credibility makes us willing to lean in and listen. Her writing is built on her experience of deep pain, and in the midst of that her rugged determination to hold on to Christ."

*Nancy Guthrie, author, **Hearing Jesus Speak into Your Sorrow***